PASSIVE INCOME IDEAS 2021

An Authentic Collection of Tested Passive Income Ideas to Make Money Online and Become Financially Independent in Today's Economy

Dylan Webb

written consent and can in no way be considered an endorsement from the trademark holder.

TABLE OF CONTENTS

INTRODUCTION

How to live on passive income?

Passive income does not mean getting something for anything. That is not possible in the real world, and the opposition believes in magic. There is always a previous work (as in writing a book, for example) or maintenance (generating income through an app, to give another example).

With this in mind and leaving aside the magic, we must also consider the following.

Most ways to generate a passive income that you see out there don't work. It's as simple as that. Or at least, they don't do it enough to be able to make a living from it or extract a return other than crumbs and pennies.

This is the real world. If there were a guaranteed or straightforward way to generate passive income, everyone would have applied it by now.

The problem is that the notion of passive income is usually, in most cases, based on the fallacy we have already discussed: that you can get something for nothing.

This does not mean that specific passive income methods are not effective. As we will see, in my experience, some of them have worked or work very well, but they have always required a significant previous work or a significant initial investment.

And most have also required maintenance, such as patching bugs in software or updating books and information that became obsolete.

Is it possible to generate 100% passive income?

It is not impossible to generate 100% passive income where we sit back on the couch, and when we look at the account, it has grown without us having to do anything. But because of that need for maintenance, pre-work, or even regular promotion to get the word out about the product that provides the passive income, someone needs to be doing that work, or the tree that bears fruit will wither.

The only way to generate 100% passive income is to have someone employed to manage, even minimally, those tasks of maintenance, updating, or advertising of the product or service.

Some systems can indeed be highly automated, but it is impossible to automate everything and sleep without everything degrading over time. From time to time, at the very least, even the most automated system will need to be reviewed and fine-tuned.

That is, if we choose to manage our wealth to optimize it and make money (one of the ways to generate a passive income that we will see), the only way to not worry about it 100% and that it works is that someone expert manages that wealth and takes a part of a salary. Or that we have set up a sound system, with stop-losses and the like, but we will have to review it from time to time.

The same happens if we have a membership site or a community (other forms that we will examine). In that case, it is advisable that someone maintains those sites, moderates the communities, or heeds the inevitable requests for support and help that there will be.

If we have someone for that, we can forget about it, and whatever is left clean after paying and maintaining costs will be 100% passive income. But if not, we will always have to do some work. Always, even if it's just a little bit.

That is the reality of passive income, and whoever tries to sell something else is trying to fool us.

It's as simple as that.

That is why many people talk about passive income when they mean "income in exchange for little work" or "income without the need to be working all the time."

For example, if we write a digital book and it sells well (another method we will examine), we will be receiving royalties long after writing that book and without us having to do anything. We can be on the couch and getting paid.

But let's not kid ourselves; in the beginning, it took a lot of work to write that book, work that now continues to pay off.

And if it's a worthwhile book, it probably took a lot of writing and a lot of late nights. Just as it is hard to make the book stand out in the sea of titles that are published every month, and we may also have had to make an effort, at least initially, to promote it.

If you want to earn more money, work less and ensure a good retirement, then it's time to start creating income streams that don't require a lot of dedication.

Passive income is within everyone's reach, young and old, as long as you come with the right mindset.

Forget the buck, and get to work with vision and perseverance.

Now it's your turn. It's your turn to sit down and start researching what passive income will allow you to spend more time with your family, take a vacation whenever you want, live in Japan if you feel like it, or sit at home generating income doing "almost" nothing.

Are you ready to give up the traditional 40-hour workweek? You "just" have to open a business with a future or create a product that generates passive income.

The longer you take to create it, the more money you will be losing.

Forget about being a slave to the clock and your schedule and start seeing money come into your pocket without you constantly having to be working.

I don't know anyone who generates passive income by reading all the time on the Internet.

So what are you going to do now?

If you're one of my kind, the ones who take action, this book will be a great help to you.

Good passive income!

The benefits of passive income

So what's so great about passive income, why is it so coveted, and what are the reasons why it appeals so much to bloggers? Well, for three straightforward reasons:

You will earn more by working less: who wants to work 40 hours a week all their life? There is a way to earn the same by working half as much. Passive income consists of generating income even if you are lying in a hammock on a Caribbean beach.

You will have the opportunity to create your lifestyle: even if you are employed or self-employed, if you offer services, you will have to adjust to schedules, deadlines, and clients. But with passive income, you can choose how to live, where and do what you want with your time. You don't have to conform to anything or anyone.

You will enjoy greater freedom: passive income gives you the freedom to not answer anyone but the clients you choose. This allows you to create the lifestyle that best fits your vision.

TYPES OF PASSIVE INCOME

If you want to understand the model better, you should know the two basic types of passive income and a third type that, while not passive income per se, can be vital to earning more while working less.

RESIDUAL INCOME

This is income that occurs over the long term and is the result of work done only once. For example, an insurance salesman receives his annual commission each time a customer renews his previously purchased policy.

A fitness instructor who launches a video sold in several gyms receives a commission for each sale—a writer who has produced an e-book and receives a profit for each copy sold. A photographer uploads his images to a digital photo bank, and every time a person downloads his photos, he receives his commission.

This type of income does not require you to be permanently active. You have to dedicate many hours of work for some time. In this, it differs from the recurring form of income, to which you must dedicate your day-to-day to charge your clients for your services.

LEVERAGED INCOME

These are the ones that allow you to take advantage of others' work that generates income for you. For example:

The author of an e-book sells his product through a network of affiliates in charge of promoting it and keeping a specific commission.

A sales team manager who receives commissions from the revenue generated by his team members.

A contractor who keeps a small margin of money from work done by subcontractors.

ACTIVE LEVERAGED INCOME

This is the third alternative I was talking about. Perhaps it doesn't quite belong to the passive income scheme as it requires your participation directly. But it has the window of allowing you to generate more income the more people you attract. Generally, this is achieved by convening events such as a training course, concerts, events, or a seminar:

Even if organizing an event is a lot of work hours, your income potential is much greater than working for someone who pays you by the hour.

The requirements for passive income

To learn how to generate passive income, it is also essential to know what a product must have to generate money passively. Some requirements have to be fulfilled to be able to obtain this type of earnings.

These requirements are:

That it is scalable: that is to say, that the income can grow and not remain stagnant. We must set the limit and not that, suddenly, this product can no longer generate more income.

Reach a large audience: if something is clear, passive income is obtained thanks to other people's flow of money. It may be through the direct purchase of a product or ad impressions and advertising on a website. Either way, you need third parties to generate your income, so you must attract many people to your business.

Automate: it is essential that, to earn money without the need for your direct work, you create automation systems that allow you to earn money even when you are at the beach. Therefore, enable payment platforms, use automation tools, and allow yourself to enjoy a much more accessible, relaxed, and economically profitable life.

If these conditions are not met, it won't be easy to generate this type of income.

How to generate passive income?

1. Create an e-book

If you are a professional in a specific field, an excellent way to generate money is to create an e-book that can be quickly sold in the digital world.

To do this, it is true that you will have to dedicate certain hours in the beginning but, later, this financial asset will be bringing you money steadily.

2. Become an influencer

Influencers are in fashion.

Thanks to social networks, there are more and more prominent people in their sector who are beginning to become relevant and followed. Therefore, to become an influencer, you will need to stand out in something and focus all your energies on that market niche.

The more followers you have, the more brands will be interested in working with you and helping you earn significant amounts of money.

3. YouTube videos or tutorials

Related to the above, another of the best ways to generate passive income is to create your own YouTube channel and gain subscribers and views.

A single video can make you a lot of money if you have a community that follows you.

It is true that, nowadays, being a YouTuber is more complicated than it seems but, with time and promotion, you can become a real crack of this social network and earn a lot of money.

4. Set up a blog

It is also one of the great panaceas of the Internet, and, increasingly, it can be more challenging to make money with this method.

However, if you find good niche pages and manage to position yourself well, you will generate income with your passion.

We have already listed above the different possibilities you have at your disposal, i.e., insert advertising, sell sponsored content, affiliate with a network such as Amazon, eBay, Alixpress, and so on.

These are just some of the ideas that can help you make money online and that the income you get is passive.

5. Online courses

This is another way to "package" your knowledge in the form of a product (productize, as the term is now so fashionable) and position it with a higher value than the book, offering it more expensive.

Everyone repeats that this is the best current way to obtain sufficient passive income. And this may be so, but again, there are several things to keep in mind.

To begin with, making a good course requires a lot of effort. Everything that was said in the book section about being real experts and not having done weekend coaching also applies in this case.

Nowadays, video is a must. Not because it makes the course better (in fact, it tends to worsen the quality, in many cases it is not the ideal format for learning and you can waste a lot of time for the students), but the current conditioning makes you expect video and quality.

A course in a format other than the video is much more challenging to sell, so that it will require investment in:

- Good camera and microphone, as well as sound production facilities.

- Additional post-production.

- Teaching skills.

- Being comfortable in front of the camera.

6. Software and downloadable products

Again, we are dealing with a product that we put some initial work into and, after completion, can continue to provide a return for a long time.

Both the marketing plan software and business plan software products have sold well throughout SMB Resources' history and are now free for any entrepreneur to take advantage of.

Today, downloadable software is being displaced by SAAS (Software as a service), which are applications, primarily web-based, that you pay for with a subscription each month (and which we'll also look at as a passive income method below).

This does not mean that downloadable software is no longer an option. Mobile apps continue to succeed and, if we are considering creating something, we should ideally look at the possibility of applying this type to have a larger market.

These two software evolutions (Software as a Service and mobile apps) are crucial to analyze in their section.

Of course, in all software forms, we will be conditioned by our IT knowledge or by the development budget we have.

7. Mobile Apps

Many programmers have been inclined to make mobile software, and it is a good move because there are many more phones than computers.

There is little to say that we don't already know, except that if we create something perfect and remarkable, a mobile app can be very similar to what we have always imagined about having passive income.

The models when it comes to monetizing our app also give us more flexibility and can be, basically:

Charge a single price per download, which is the traditional software model.

Make it free, but with advertising. This would be the closest way to the passive income that we all have in mind. We will see more about the general issue of such passive income in exchange for advertising.

Make it free, but with paid premium options or microtransactions to get advantages, something ubiquitous in games.

Charge a monthly subscription, whereby we have turned the app into a SAAS.

Either way, it has the same advantages and disadvantages that we have already seen. It will require watching out for bugs, updating the application often, adding new features...

8. Investing in companies, start-ups, and other initiatives

This passive income method is a variant of the above in which we invest directly in a new company by contributing capital, or we participate as partners in other business ventures.

If we are only capitalist partners, thanks to that money, we will obtain passive income in annual profit-sharing, the possible sale of company shares once they have appreciated, etc.

This is a method that can be 100% passive.

9. Product licensing

This is another method used in SMB Resources over perfect time and the closest thing to the notion of passive income that we all have in mind.

It is based on the following.

You create a product (usually software, but it doesn't have to be, it can also be information or a method or way of doing things) and, instead of selling it yourself directly, you license it to another company to use or sell it and offer it to their audience.

On many occasions, that company will want to offer it with their branding on the product, so you offer something "white label" that they adopt as their own.

For example, in SME Resources, Zen Marketing software was being offered many years ago to various corporate training companies for their teaching curricula.

There was a white label version in which the client's branding was put on and, each month, they would order the number of licenses they needed, and the codes were generated here, which they gave to their students so they could access the software.

They offered it as an incentive in their courses, and from here, the license was sold at a lower price than the RRP but compensated by the good number of monthly licenses obtained without doing anything special.

Undoubtedly, if I had to talk about the most profitable passive income method in my case, it would be this one. The collaboration with training companies and consulting firms was perfect for a few years.

I insist that software is the most common thing in licensing, but it is not the only thing. Over time I have licensed information or even working methods.

10. Dropshipping stores

I was not going to comment on this form of "passive income" because it does not deserve it. But then I thought it is essential to do so as a warning and clarify these things' reality.

This "passive income" model has become famous because some social networks are flooded with young people's ads showing a lot of money and saying that they have obtained it thanks to a "simple system" that hardly requires any work.

It is called dropshipping.

Dropshipping is very old, and those older than us have been seeing it almost since the beginning of the Internet.

The business model is based on creating an online store that is an intermediate showcase of products that manage another company in stock, payments, and shipments.

In other words, you put this online storefront, you attract visitors, they buy, and it is the dropshipping company that manages the stock, the order, and the shipping.

In reality, this magical method of passive income translates into creating and maintaining intermediary websites that do not add value and only inflate the price of a cheap and poor-quality product.

Affiliate Marketing Tips

1. You Need to Be Patient.

We all know that things take time, but by following these tips, and everything else you learn in these series, you'll give yourself the best options to make things happen as fast as it possibly takes for you with affiliate marketing.

So take action and keep learning as you go, because it is not just a walk in the park.

No matter how quick people say that you can make money online, realize that it will take time. Yes, things can happen pretty fast—that's the beauty of the online business world.

You can have a site up today and start sharing content with the world, but to make an impact and earn money online, you're going to need to get your message out there and build relationships with clients. This will drive some traffic to your site in no time and eventually clicks, sales, and affiliate commissions.

2. Making A Product Instead

Affiliate marketing doesn't always work out how we would expect it to, in some intendance, and there are advantages to creating your products. You will get to keep people in your brand. You will get to keep all the profits. You can even set up your affiliate programs for other people to sign up and promote your products.

This isn't affiliate marketing. And even when you create your product, you'll waive the benefits of affiliate marketing, such as not creating the product, dealing with customer service, and other aspects of being a product owner.

If all collateral fails, you will know there's a market out there for a particular product that's perfect for your audience, and it doesn't exist, create it yourself.

3. Testing

Testing your offers, yes, but more than that—testing everything else. Test how you promote, to view what your audience responds best to. Test the placements of your links, the number of links within the posts; whether they're bolded or italicized, whether images are working better, whether interviewing the owner helps, whether Tuesday's convert better than Thursday's for webinars ... test everything you can think of.

4. Also Try Other Offers

It's all a learning process, one that happens through taking action and trials and errors.

That's what affiliate marketing is all about.

The more things don't work out, the better, and because it's, the more likely, you'll be to get to something that does work eventually. And the more you'll keep learning along the way.

I am figuring out why you can evaluate the circumstances and try again, knowing what you now know from what you have learned. Then use what you have learned and tried another offer!

It's not the end of the world. Sometimes you'll think that your audience will respond one way, but they'll surprise you and go the opposite way. The campaign you thought was going to be a home run turns out to be a bust.

Let's just say you have an affiliate product that you'd like to promote. You've used the product, it's fantastic, and you know that it will help your audience. You set up a promotion with links in your posts, create an epic post with videos, the whole 9 yards . . . and surprisingly, it doesn't work out.

5. Believe in Your Recommendation

If your audience will believe in you and if you believe in that particular product, in your recommendation, and then in your audience, If you motives other than trying to help people out or give them something that they need—if it's for the commission, or you're just doing a favor for a friend who owns a product—then you're not going to perform well with your sales at all.

6. Focus on How It Can Help Your Audience and Benefit from It

Whenever you're talking about a product to your audience, it doesn't matter which platform you're using or methods you choose to deliver your content; always focus more on your audience's benefits. In other words, what's in it for them?

In each section of your blog posts, in your videos, podcast episodes, don't forget to remind your audience exactly how that product will help them.

Benefits are what people need. It's pretty cool that this link building tool can help you to get links from high Ranked Page sites, but the benefit is that your site will have more authority, so you'll rank higher in Google and get more traffic."

it's cool that this in-ear headphone comes with a flat, tangle-free wire, but the benefit is that you don't get easily frustrated trying to untangle the darn thing every time you take it out of your bag or pocket."

If you're having trouble with this whole feature vs. benefit thing, that's okay—a lot of people will get confused, but the most straightforward ways are to understand it so you can learn more about it.

7. Ask for A Landing Page on The Owner's Site

The big caution is this will not always be possible, which is why it's an advanced tip. Some companies are not open to creating a custom landing page for you, and even if they are, you need to be a successful affiliate with them already before they agree to it.

This landing page's significant benefit is that it continues the conversation and makes the customer feel like you're still there with them as they're going through the purchase process.

When individuals click on your affiliate link, they're taken to a custom landing page on the company's site that has some elements from your brand on it. Another more comfortable option that can increase your audience's trust and comfort in purchasing is having your own branded landing page on the company's site.

In some cases, you will be able to handle the purchase process on your site, but that requires the company agreed to do it, along with a lot of technical knowledge on how to do it.

Getting the final product and the company goes ahead, you can help ensure that your audience will have a positive purchasing experience. But you're still sending your audience into another company's "territory" where you don't usually have any control over their experience.

In most cases, an affiliate item's actual sale occurs on the company's website that owns the actual product. Unfortunately, it's complicated to keep all sales processing on your site, so you'll need to be willing to send people to the company's site to complete their purchase.

8. Offer Special Deals Just for Audience

I've done special deals on several products with Convert kit, and each time it has driven the affiliate sales through the roof. You're able to do a limited-time deal or one that is evergreen.

This is the next step of building a relationship with the owner of a product that you're promoting. If you can negotiate a special deal from the product owner just for your audience, then that will give your audience an even better value and more of a reason to purchase from you. Try to work out a deal with the product owner before you have them as a guest on your podcast. What's the worst that could happen? They'll say no, that's all.

9. Establish A Relationship with The Owner of The Product

The advantage of building a relationship with the product owners is you might even be able to make negotiable or higher commission rates. You are making a connection that is worth it!

I have a great relationship with the team at Convert kit as well. Because I've cultivated this relationship, I've had the option to speak at their event, and they've let me offer a longer free trial time that my audience seems to appreciate.

I have established that relationship with the Convert kit team, even having meetings at their offices to meet the team. Not just to get to know them, but to ensure they're on top of things and helping out my audience, learning about new product plans that are coming up that I will help promote that could be a win for both, and see if there's anything else they can do to help make my life easier, such as creating customized landing pages.

This does a few things. One of them is it starts to foster the necessary relationship and trust between your audience and the product owner if your audience is ever going to purchase any of the products. Second, it helps the audience to trust you even more by showing them that you've established a relationship with the owner of the product, and you're not just messing around when it comes to recommending the product. You're even more familiar with the product and the people behind it, which will help your audience feel comfortable with their purchase.

If You're promoting a product and get the product owner to answer some questions about it, which you have posted in a blog post, or a podcast episode, or maybe a video interview of that sort. Or maybe you have that individual on as a guest, and he or she offers you some high-value content, with a small promo for the product at the end, which I think would be fantastic.

10. Review and Compare Different Products of The Same Types.

The reason that this works is that people like shopping around, but they also like convenience. Instead of making them carry out their search all over the web, keep them on your site by reviewing each of the different products in one spot. If you've done a great job building up audience trust, then it's a well-written comparison to reviews of other products of the same type, which can be a great way to drive affiliate purchases. This could potentially become an epic post, complementary with videos and special deals just for your audience.

Another strategy is to compare other products of the same type. Compare and contrast, if you give them your recommendation, make sure that the link is an affiliate link.

11. Promote Products Indirectly on Other People's Sites

This is another instance in which indirect linking is your friend. If you're interviewed for another person's blog or asked to write a guest post, you can link back to a piece of content on your site containing your affiliate link. As for social media and email, you don't want to hit people over the head with your links most of the time. If you're trying to link directly to an affiliate product through someone else's site, they won't allow it anyway.

12. Promote Products Indirectly Via Your Email List

The email list should be all about giving people as much high-value content as possible, not direct selling. Specific affiliate programs such as Craigslist don't even allow you to include affiliate links in emails.

You'll need to take good care of your email list and not to be too aggressive with it. Indirect promotion is a much better way to go about things, especially if you're focused on building trust with your audience.

As for social media, I recommend indirectly promoting your email list.

I don't directly promote anything on my email list. If there are any links in my emails, they usually point back to other content, usually on my blog, such as Podcasts, videos, webinars, and others alike.

Your email list is an integral part of any affiliate marketing campaign, and if you don't have one, you need to get started building one today! An email list is compelling for marketing.

13. Run A Giveaway to Take Advantage of Social Proof

I've used this strategy to achieve great success in promoting several products in the past, so I'd suggest you give it a shot.

You can also follow up with the individual who leaves a comment on the post but doesn't win, share a limited-time deal or an email saying thanks for the entry and giving them your affiliate link one more time again.

What happens here is that you get tons of people leaving comments that become social proof for the product's greatness. There's nothing more powerful than someone else's recommendation and testimony, and in this case, it is other people's recommendation for a product that you're promoting as an affiliate.

You can promote your affiliate links in a blog post, review the product—maybe it's your epic post, or you can just mention it at the end of one of your regular posts.

Also, share that you have two or three copies of the product to give away for free, and they'll have to order to enter to win one of the copies; your audience has to leave a comment about how they would use the product would help them.

Then let them go through an affiliate link of yours to see what the product is all about first, and then come back to your blog to leave their entry as a comment.

If you ever plan to promote a product as an affiliate, and if possible, work with the owner to get a few copies to give away to your audience for free. Also, if possible, get a discounted price for a limited time for your audience as well. It may not always be possible, but you can always ask to see what happens. This is how the strategy will play out in the real world.

Online, this translates to have other people doing the marketing for you, except in this case, it's through metrics like depending on the number of subscribers, likes, comments. Social proof is an idea that people will naturally gravitate toward what the masses are doing. As an example, let's say you're at the mall, and you see a big crowd gathering around a store. You can't help but want to know what's going on, why is everyone else there, and for some reason, and you want to know what that reason is for all this.

14. Promote Your Products Indirectly on Social Media

One of the cardinal rules of online marketing has long been that the fewer doorway or clicks people have to go through before they can click the buy button, the better it is.

But I think that is changing, and now it's getting closer to the less information you give away, the less you're likely to make a sale.

The more trust you can earn initially, the greater the likelihood people will buy from you.

You don't want someone to have to click a thousand times before they get to where you want them to go, but a few clicks are okay, as long as you give them enough information at the beginning to help them make their decision.

If you're not linking directly through your affiliate link, but a resource that will engage people at the beginning, earn their trust, and show them what the product is about before clicking on your affiliate link.

But all is not lost in the affiliate marketing world because you can do an indirect social media push start, which means instead of directly linking to your affiliate links on Instagram, Facebook, or Twitter, or any other platform, you're instead linking to something of value that includes the affiliate link, such as a video, an epic post on your blog, or a link to sign up for a webinar.

The thing about social media is, at least from my experience and in the experience of many other people, I know that if you're directly promoting on your social media platforms, you're not going to get a good response. People on social media are there to be social, not to be sold to.

All through your website is the centerpiece of your affiliate marketing strategy, social media, Instagram, Facebook, Twitter, LinkedIn, Instagram, etc.—can play an essential role in your affiliate marketing strategy.

15. Give Away A Bonus

Making your buyers feel pleased and helping them get those on the fence from "I'm not sure if this is right for me at all" to saying this is precisely what I need, and the more you're adding value to the purchase.

Maybe the bonus is a product or piece of software that you have to complements the affiliate product. Maybe it's a discount price that you work out with the product owner, which provides an incentive to purchase from you. Maybe it's a coupon code or discount to another product that you own or have ties to. Maybe it's a PDF quick-start guide with instructions and best practices for that product, or access to a website with videos that as the same guidance.

Maybe it's a special webinar that shows people how to use the product with a question and answer session at the end of it. Imagine being able to purchase a product, getting familiar with it, and then a few days later having access to a webinar that shows you exactly how to use the product, with an opportunity to ask questions about it. How awesome would that be?

16. Publish A Webinar Replay

I will recommend you a recording using screen capture software like Screen flow or Camtasia Studio.

The truth is more people will probably watch it as a replay than a live show, and that's a good thing. You have to allow them to do so.

Be sure to record your live webinar so that you can embed it on your website as a replay for those who didn't watch it live and those who did watch it live but like the option to review the information.

You are making sure that in the webinar and on the post where you embed the replay, you give individuals the opportunities to click on your affiliate link multiple times.

17. Host A Webinar

Having the product owner share high-value information and even answering people's questions directly on the webinar, and you'd make yourself a winner.

Webinars are a compelling way for you to share a message with your audience.

They're personable, they're alive, and you can treat them like an event.

That way, your promotion becomes a much bigger deal than just a regular affiliate link that you dropped into a post and take your affiliate product promotion to the next level.

18. Create Multiple YouTube Videos About the Product

I will recommend you record yourself from start to finish with it, and then break it up into smaller portions.

People like to watch short videos, so this will work in your favor, and you get multiple opportunities to rank for various keywords related to that product.

Whether it's a digital product, start at the moment of purchase and walk people through the entire procedure.

And if you happen to be doing a physical product, consider an unboxing video.

Your videos should be embedded in the epic post. This is an essential strategy because YouTube is the second search engine that we have in the world.

You can get a lot of traffic coming in through your affiliate links on YouTube, and the videos themselves can rank in Google as well. Also, by shooting multiples videos about a particular product, you'll create even more SEO opportunities. Make sure to include your affiliate link in the video description, especially in the first part of the description, so people don't have to click on show more, or read more, to see it.

19. Create an Epic Post

I love to do it when I'm promoting a product because I create an Epic Post about it. What's an epic post? How about thinking of it as a potential one-stop-shop resource for this particular product and not just a review of it, but a full-fledged introduction, how-to, FAQ, best practices, and troubleshooting resource for anyone that purchases the product? If you can show all this information to people before making a purchase, they'll be more likely to purchase that product. Simultaneously, the epic post becomes an extremely shareable article, one with the potential to rank high for the particular product keyword in Google or SEO.

20. Thank People After for Going Through Your Affiliate Links

If the company's tracking system you're an affiliate with should show you the name or emails of people who purchase through your link, you would follow up with those people and thank them. Maybe give them a little surprise bonus if you want to, something that you didn't mention, they'd get in the first place. This will help to make them want to purchase through one of your affiliate links.

21. Thank People in Advance for Going Through Your Affiliate Link

Whenever I disclose my affiliate links on my blog posts or videos, I sometimes thank people for going through them. Is this a small thing that probably wouldn't make a drastic difference in accumulating sales? Yes. It is easy to do, and people will appreciate it, of course.

22. Use Your Language to Promote Your Affiliate Link

However, when you sign up as an affiliate with a company, they'll often send you marketing languages to use in your emails, blog posts, and social media messages to help sell the product.

While this language can be helpful, I recommend that you not use it 100 percent verbatim.

Try to use it as an inspiration to craft personalized language to sell the products, And Why?

Because you want your audience to trust you, your audience wants to hear from you in your voice. It will be evident to them if you're copying from somewhere else.

23. Keep Track of Your Click-Through

If you have just one affiliate link for every direction your videos, podcasts, blog posts, webinars, etc.— then how do you know where you're getting most of your sales from? How would you know what campaigns aren't working and which ones aren't?

This takes a lot of time to set up, but you have to know what's happening to each of your links to understand what is working and what isn't. You need to track it.

One of the things you should always do with your affiliate links is to keep track of them, where they are located in your content, how many clicks are going through each portal, and your conversion rates.

24. Disclose That Your Links Affiliate Links

When the time mentioned that you're using affiliate links, you should also say you're getting a commission, but at no extra cost for them, so if they are going to buy the product anyway, they might as well buy it from you and help you make some money as well.

But even more than that, people appreciate honesty. Along with that, if you give away enough information and help people out, some of those same people more and likely would want to pay you back for your generosity. If you disclose that you have an affiliate link that they can click on, that right there is an excellent call to action for people to give back to you.

Well, at least in the US, Federal Trade Commission regulations require that if you're receiving any compensation for promoting any other product or company, you have to disclose that sort of relationship. There's a lot more to it than that, but the best thing you can do is be honest and upfront with your links.

Well, most of you know that I'm all about transparency and authenticity, and it's no different with affiliate links at all. So, I will do my best always to reveal that links are affiliate links.

25. Give People Multiple Opportunity to Clink on Your Affiliate links

Is another quick and easy tip is to link product images with your affiliate link. If you think of adding affiliate links to other content, it is as easy as possible for your visitors to use your affiliate links without overdoing it.

You can catch the "low-hanging fruit" with your first link (since many people will click on it just because it's there). But the people who continue to read the post are likely to be more engaged and take action. That's where adding your links in the middle and at the end can come in handy, so they can engage readers that they don't have to scroll back up the page.

You should avoid doing it exceptionally as well. You will go overboard with stuffing affiliate links into your posts. The best thing to do is just naturally place links where it seems like it will work. For a blog post, this could be the first time you have mentioned the product, somewhere in the middle of the post, and then again at the end.

I say "sadly" because many people are missing out on the potential income as a result. When you're only allowing your audience to click on your affiliate link just by adding a single link near the top of a blog post, for example, you're just losing out on the potential income that could come with not much work that many people fail to implement.

26. Use Your Website

There are enough tools available that allow you to do everything without a website, but if you're in it for the long pull and want to do affiliate marketing the right way, you need to have a website. Why would you ever want to put your business in the hands of somebody else?

The smart approach is to create a website where you have full control over your audience and customers' experience. Platforms like Instagram and Facebook are limited when delivering a custom experience to your audience.

Twitter is extremely more limited. LinkedIn and YouTube are limited in customer experience, and you would want those places to be the start of a conversation and always drive people back to your website.

The website is where all the actions happen. It is where people purchase stuff. It's where people click and share things mostly, and it's where you can get the most leveraging. It's where you can most easily develop an email list.

Affiliate marketing is your business, and that's why you need to take control of it, and if you put your business in the hands of Instagram, Facebook, Twitter, or even Google, you're risking everything.

When it comes to affiliate marketing, one of those is a must-have: a website. I know many people generating passive income via Instagram, Facebook, Twitter, LinkedIn, and YouTube, without even having a website. This is The Power to them all, but if you want to set yourself up for success with affiliate marketing, you'll need a website. What if Facebook or Twitter were to shut down today? That probably won't happen anytime soon, but these sites can still make changes that significantly affect your business. We've seen this over and over again, especially with Facebook. Facebook loves to make changes, mostly since they went public and tried to make money for their investors.

There are many ways to develop an audience today: on social media like Facebook, Twitter, or Instagram, or your website.

27. Become A Source Of Information And Support For A Product

A lot of people think that "NO" they don't want any emails from people about their affiliate products." You should because the people who email you other than everyone else are the ones who are most interested in being successful with a product.

If you're worried this means you'll be deluged with support emails, don't be afraid! You're not going to be burned with questions. In all my years of experience offering support for my affiliate products, I've never had a problem receiving too many questions. But the value of offering support is enormous and will help your audience to trust your recommendations.

The next thing you can do is provide support for it as well. You don't necessarily have to be available all the time for customer service questions.

But when you promote these products, you will want to say, "Hey, if you have any questions about this, please let me know.

Because I know of this product, and I want to show you how it can help you to achieve your goals or addressing your pains and problems." And when you do that, your audience will automatically think, "That this guy knows what he's talking about, and if in case I ever have any questions, "he is there."

It may just take an answer to a simple question to get the person to click through your link and make a purchase. They'll feel more secure with their purchase, again, since they'll know if they have any questions, they can then come to you.

If someone has any questions about a product before making a purchase, tell them to go through you (or maybe someone on your staff or a virtual assistant).

The next level is to make yourself available to your audience as a source of information and support for that product, to treat the product as your own.

28. Help Your Audience Learn As Much As Possible About The Product

The Link for a product that you recommend on one of your sites, giving your audience thorough information about a product like this that will help you become a source of information, the more you can show, the more comfortable people will be whenever making a purchase.

Instead of just a paragraph or two explaining the product and what it can do for them, it shows them how it works and the benefits.

Tell them what it is like to sign up for the product, share some tips to make the experience of using the product even better, give answers to the most frequently asked questions about that product showing them everything. So a person sees an affiliate

29. Show Your Results

By showing that I've used and succeeded with a product like Convert kit, which helps to build that trust and lessen the "I don't know exactly what this product is about, so I'm not even going to buy it" mentality among the audience.

For example, the tool that I've called Convert Kit helps me run my email campaigns to build an even bigger following. I then also use my results as proof when promoting Convert Kit as an affiliate product to my audience.

One of the most significant ways that I've been able to take my affiliate income to the next level is by showing people what I've gained from using those products.

30. Can I Trust This Product? Will It Be Good For My Audience

The moment you decide to promote something as an affiliate, you attach yourself to a brand and your business to that company and that product, and if that product isn't going to be suitable for your audience, then it's going to reflect on you eventually. I was once approached to promote a product that I knew would sell well and make me a lot of money. But I didn't promote it because I wouldn't say I liked how the company managed the upsell procedure, which was very aggressive, and ended with an automatic 30-day trial. That didn't sit well with me, so I didn't promote it. I may have lost some money upfront because of that decision, but it was still the right thing to do in the long run. If it's terrible, it's a lose-lose-lose for everybody.

If it's a fantastic product that helps them out, that's awesome! You're going to look at that much better and be thanked for it, and it will be a win-win-win for everyone.

This is crucial. It's the idea that you would be sharing or recommending something that will help your audience. Do you trust that after you send people through your link that the sales page for that product, I mean the product itself, and the customer service for that product, if any, will be useful to them?

31. Know the Product

If you're not too familiar with a product, do not promote it. It may not be a rule most affiliate marketers follow, but it's the one I've followed for years with great success because it helps build that trust fact with my audience.

Don't get me wrong, it's smart for a marketer to consider what the commission is and how much money you earn per sale, but the commission shouldn't drive you to promote a product. It should be just one part of the whole decision to promote a product. So, know the product. Because if you know the product, it will shape how you promote it, what you say to promote it, and the overall feeling people will get when you offer or recommend it.

One of the biggest mistakes that I often see people make when attempting to sell a product as an affiliate does not know much about the product. This usually stems from a desire to push a product for the primary purpose of earning money from it, which doesn't work like that.

31. Build Trust First

Relationships with other individuals are significant to having success, and you won't have sustainable success with your affiliate marketing until you earn your audience's trust.

Recommendations from others getting on other people's radar and have them doing the marketing for you. Not for the affiliate products that you're promoting, but you or your brand.

Your trust is earned faster through the friends and relationships that people already have with each other.

That's why it's essential to give to everyone, no matter how big or small it may seem to your brand.

Because you'll never know—they may know somebody who knows somebody who will become your biggest client, or a multi-product customer, or maybe the window of opportunity that would have never happened otherwise.

You are giving away as much as possible; free content information, free high-value stuff, and sometimes even your own time. Online karma does exist, and the more you give away, the more you will get back in return—and sometimes it's not even from the very same people you gave to, which is why the second piece of earning is trust.

My number one tip is to build trust! Trust takes time to develop and the energy to maintain it.

This is why I give you these tips because I don't want you to expect things to happen overnight; it takes a while and focuses on building your community and the trust within that community first.

The recommendation for products and the affiliate love you'll get from your community comes almost naturally after you EARN that trust from them.

Thankfully, you can do things to increase the number of people clicking on your affiliate links and buying the affiliate products you're promoting.

Affiliate marketing is not a "push-button" problem solution.

It takes focus and commitment, and specific choreography makes it happen the way you want to see it. It can also be a beautiful thing when it works— in a win-win-win for all parties! Affiliate marketing is just simple in concept.

Some Tips on How You Can Make Money with YouTube

1. You Might Be Thinking

Can you make real money with YouTube? Are you going to generate a passive income by depending on impression-based ad revenue? Probably not; as an alternative, you need to identify ways in which you can leverage YouTube's network to accomplish revenue streams.

2. Transition Into live Speaking Engagements.

Live speaking engagements can be very profitable. It's possible to generate passive income from just an hour-long presentation.

So make sure that you're seeking out these opportunities. And never ignore the chance of growing your audience.

In the end, leverage your YouTube reputation and attract live speaking engagements. If the YouTube channel that you produce is focused on a specific niche or audience, do some research about annual conferences or other industry events that have keynotes speakers. Then, use your YouTube statistics and some of your best clips to put together a package and pitch to these events' directors.

3. Attract Sponsorships.

The good thing about sponsorships is that you don't have to give YouTube a cut. You can negotiate whatever contracts you want based on your impressions and the size of your audience. In most instances, the revenue that you generate from sponsorships is substantially more than YouTube ad revenues. Meanwhile, you can still generate ad revenue. So it's more like to have two sources of income from the same video.

If you study the most successful YouTube's, you'll notice the number of sponsorships and advertisements in their video recordings. These deals are opportunities that the video-makers have generated by themselves.

4. Direct Traffic to Affiliate Links.

Instead of depending on static blogs to direct people to your affiliate links, try creating a lively YouTube channel and use it as the primary catalyst. As the internet continues to maneuver toward video as the primary form of content, you can get ahead of the curve and start reaping the rewards to benefit now.

Affiliate marketing is a hugely popular online money-making opportunity. The issue is that so many affiliate marketers don't put forth the effort it takes to generate a sizable income.

5. Sell Premium Videos with Yondo.

One of the best ways to do this is by using a solution called Yondo, which is used to create your store that sells on-demand that particular video content with your domain. You can sell pay per view rentals, and monthly subscriptions, or anything in between. Best of all, you'll get to set your price, and you don't have to split revenue down the middle with YouTube at all.

If your goal is to make money from videos, there's a far better option than merely depending on your measly allocation of ad revenue. Instead, you can create a YouTube channel and build an audience. The primary goal is to engage this audience and build a brand name. Then, once you've established a reputation, start driving traffic to your landing pages where you can up-sell viewers with premium video content.

6. Sell Your Goods with Shopify.

There is a lot more to it than this, but it's what the conversion channel looks like for all intents and purposes. If you have the right product and your videos are engaging and straightforward, this channel will work almost every time.

Let's assume that you already have a product to sell. You can set it up an e-commerce storefront using a resource like Shopify, then produce videos that fit into your product's niche. At the end of the video, you can produce a calculated call to action that drives traffic to your product landing pages.

YouTube is the second-largest search engine globally, followed by Google from a marketing point of view; it doesn't make sense to ignore this significant resource. One of the best money-making opportunities is that you can use YouTube to sell your physical products.

To earn passive income from YouTube is to stop viewing that the platform is a monetize-able medium in and of itself.

For instance, think of YouTube as a catalyst.

The real way to earn money from YouTube is to leverage its massive network.

That's how you'll make money with YouTube.

7. The Challenges of Making Money from YouTube

In other words, you're only going to make a few thousand dollars for every million views. And, make no doubt about it; getting millions of views is very challenging. The good news is that YouTube ads aren't the only revenue-generating opportunities for creative individuals willing to work hard and develop actual business plans.

Even if advertisers pay a decent amount to promote their products through video ads, only a portion of their expenditures ever make it into content creators' pockets. For example, if advertisers are paying an average of $10 per 1,000 ad impressions, the videos where those ads have been showing may only generate $1 or $2 per 1,000 views."

The YouTube myth goes like this: Post some videos attract many viewers and then cash in on the revenue generated from ads. It sounds easy, effortless, and straightforward, so that's the story everyone regularly uses to sell get-rich-quick schemes. However, the reality is that you cannot earn passive income based on YouTube ad revenue alone.

To make money from YouTube, you have to dig into it a little deeper and establish a more sustainable strategy.

You'll consistently see that platform's name come up to the top in articles about making money from home. Yet, while you can certainly make money with YouTube, that objective is not usually achieved in the traditional manner everyone wants you to believe.

How Photography Tips Make Money

Leave out photos that contain lens flare or vegetating in corners of the sky. Or fix the vegetating in Photoshop before submitting it.

Do not crop any of your first ten images tightly. Leave space around the main subject. Do not submit square or odd size images. And again, this comes down to the marker's preference, so best not to do it initially.

Those first ten application images don't use photos of public places, people, or human-made objects. These are often rejected due to various copyright issues.

Make sure there are no trademarks or brand names seen in the scenery. It is easy to miss small brands that may appear in the background of a photo.

Do not try to wow them with anything fancy, to begin with. For example, don't submit images of panning with cars. Leave that for when you're accepted. Again, play it safe. Usually a few boring ones, but a safe shot is the best.

To be safe when applying, do not submit popular subjects like flowers (as seen above), dogs, or water drops. They have a high option of being rejected simply because they have enough of those subjects in their database already. Once you are accepted by Shutter stock, and then submit all the photos that you like. The hardest part of Shutter stock is getting in.

Do not choose ten images all from the same theme. For example, don't have two or three different types of the same animal in numerous positions. Just choose the best of each subject. Otherwise, they could get rejected for duplicate images.

Then you can create an account with [Shutter stock](#) or another stock photography company.

For all stock photography companies, you'll need to submit a sample portfolio of several photos.

My tips on getting these initial photos approved:

As I've learned, focusing on niche content and keyword hash-tags to boost photo visibility in various search engines is more critical in stock photography than spending hours getting the perfect shot.

That's not to say that time consuming and ultra-high quality photography isn't worth anything at all. It is just not as efficient to sell on most stock photography sites. These images need to be sold directly to marketing agencies and end-users to receive their fair payment.

Perhaps even better, as I've learned, there is such a tremendous demand for virtually any stock photography and everything that you do not need "stunning" photos of exotic places to get downloads.

Some of the best photos (taken with a high-quality professional camera) have never even sold once from my experience, while random photos snapped with my iPhone have sold multiple times!

With these types of smartphones having such sophisticated cameras, it is possible to submit photos from your day-to-day life, licensed as stock photography.

When evaluating any passive income idea, it's essential to look for any unforeseen costs or blockages. It used to be extremely expensive to own professional photography equipment when it comes to stock photography, and it's very time consuming to upload photos.

In this way, a single photo could represent a residual income opportunity since it can be sold repeatedly. You'll simply need to create your photo portfolio, upload images to the photo platform, and then the activity becomes completely passive. All the technicalities of photo sales are handled through the website's platform.

You'll simply collect a check (or PayPal payment) every month for the royalties you'll receive on your photos.

Photography websites such as Shutter stock provide you with platforms to sell your photos. They may offer either a percentage or a flat fee for each photo sold to a site client.

Don't you just like photography; do you have a smartphone with a camera? If so, you're able to convert your photos into a passive income source of selling your photos as a photographer.

Car Rental Tips

UpScale

Scalability is essential in this idea. Once you have a scale of 5+ cars, the pressure rises, and you'll have to keep track of all these cars and rentals. I've agreed with a parking lot to house all my cars. When renters land or go to pick up, my attendants handle all of the transfer work, including taking pictures of any damage and handing over the keys. Also, I couldn't have done this without my partners, who also invested in this idea.

Making A few Thousands

You need to scour the internet for good deals on cars. I will share a deal that I took advantage of. It is now dead, so there's no point in looking for it again.

In December 2016, it was possible to lease a Chevy Cruise for $18/per month with $0 down.

There was no catch that it was real, and I added multiple Chevy Cruzes to my "fleet." You would need to have a pre-existing lease, but the payment went up to $60/month even if you didn't. The terms were 10,000 miles a year for two years for a total of 20,000 miles over twenty-four months. The total cost: $700 with tax, title, license out the door, which coincidentally was refunded to me because Costco was giving out $700 gift cards if you bought a Cruise at that time. There was also a monthly fee of $18, which I also paid fully in advance. Also, my monthly insurance on the car is about $8. I don't know how that happened, but it did. I also sit around and always look for new lease deals as well in my free time.

Now imagine leasing a Chevy Cruise for $18/per month and renting it out for $35/day. You don't have to imagine it because that's pretty much exactly what I'm doing.

Here's the math:

Chevy Cruise

Daily/Weekly/Monthly Rates: $35/$169/$550

Profit

After Fees: 25% = ~$27/$127/$412

Profit Margins Average per Cruse: 2,500%

A big question that's on your mind might be; what happens if you go over miles on a lease?

Answer: On the Cruse, I am making an instant profit. After the first month, I have quite literally paid off for the entire car lease – a 2500% profit in one month more than pays off 24 months of payments. The average monthly miles racked up is around 3,000. With that calculation, I will hit 20,000 miles during month 7. The day I hit 20,000 miles, I will simply give the car back or park it at my house for the next thirteen months. The car would have made me a profit by two months at the latest, so I have nothing to worry about. Even at the bare minimum of $400/per month in profit, I will have made $2,400 per Cruse. The numbers are closer to $600-800/per month, though, because most people rent for 3-4 days at $35/day versus the $169/week or $550/month.

Customer Service

Depending on what type of cars you rent out, the type of people will also vary. If you rent out cheaper cars, expect lower-income renters to rent from you. In the past, this has caused an issue for me because some people will try to find faults with anything and ask for reimbursement. The same applies to higher-income renters and high tech vehicles. They will bring their tire tread depth tools to make sure the car is perfect. If it isn't, be prepared to reimburse! I notice that I'm made aware of more trivial "issues" on my base level of vehicles versus my higher-tech ones. As I just started renting out more base-level cars, this trend is pretty new to me, and I'm not quite sure I know exactly how to deal with it as yet! Be prepared to respond to them when leaving feedback rationally.

For years, you have been on the receiving end of customer service.

Whether it was dealing with a clueless agent when booking awards or calling for retention offers, customer service was my key for me.

That is why you need to make it essential for your renters.

Simply put, if you are rude and don't care at all about people, don't rent out cars.

Remember that this app mainly exists because people are fed up with high prices and robotic customer services offered by major rental companies.

You are a human and need to act like one when renting your cars out. I cannot stress this enough!

If a renter is running 30 minutes late, there is no reason to charge a late fee. Not only will you lose that renter for life but also you might get a bad review.

If you get many bad reviews, you'll either be kicked off the platform, or people just won't rent from you.

You need to be the person that understands that issues may arrive and can deal with them appropriately.

Preference

It is imperative to list your pickup instructions.

I will not stress this enough.

Most renters skipped grades from 1-7 and forgot how to read instructions. If your car address and pickup address are different, you'll need to make that clear.

When I say clear, I meant it should be the first sentence in your description. Even though you'll have the occasional, some fools will still ask you where to pick up the car.

They will also allow you to organize an option on how to deliver the vehicle to the renter for an additional fee.

I really wouldn't recommend this for any amount because the first month of deliveries always sucked the soul out of me.

No amount of money will make me want to deliver another car again!

I put $50 for delivery, but that is only to cover either paying someone to drop my car off with Task Rabbit (an app that outsources small jobs to people who are willing to do them) or sending a Huber for the renter to come to pick up the car. However, you should set a delivery price for all major airports nearest to you because the bulk of your rentals will come from individuals flying in.

Setting advance notice is essential because this will determine how soon a renter can book your car. You can set it as soon as three hours or as far as a few days. I set mine to three hours because most people who use this app are last-minute travelers who can't find a good deal with traditional car rental companies.

The importance of clarifying the mileage limits on your description.

You'd need to charge 80 cents per mile over the allotted limit, but I'm usually not a perfectionist for miles, and I usually let renters go 30-35 miles over before charging them.

Even if I charge them, I tend to ask them to pay me for the miles in cash increments of $25/100 miles over the limit.

It is much more reasonable and makes the renters feel at ease.

While doing a little research, I found that my cars are driven MUCH less when I set them to unlimited versus setting a mileage limit.

When individuals are paying for something and are given a limit, they try to get as close to it as they possibly can. It's just human nature to maximize — you'd try getting the maximum amount for your money too! My theory is that if the car is set to unlimited, individuals don't usually go out of their way to drive the car more and just forget about it.

It is up to you to set a maximum mileage on your cars. Usually, on more high-end cars, the mileage should be set to 150 miles/per day, 1000 miles/per week, and 1500 miles/per month.

On more basic vehicles, I'll just leave it at unlimited miles. This won't happen to work that great on cars that you lease with low mileage leases except for some conditions I explained above.

Calendar

You can change the price of your car daily if needed. This is important because, through previous research, we have noticed that people will pay more on weekends for a leisure car versus the weekly renters who need your car for some other reasons. If you have a more expensive car, you can go ahead and change the price on the weekends from $20-50 higher per day.

Holiday weekends are also known for price increases. Use your supplies and demand to your advantage.

It is essential to look at your calendar featuring the app and mark the days that the car won't be available. If you're able to make the car available every day, once someone rents the car, the featured app will automatically block out the times, so you don't have to.

It's essential to extend the unavailability by an hour, maybe just if the renter shows up late or something. If you don't, the app will rent your car out at the immediate drop off time that was featured from the past rental, and that can cause the second customer to be sad about having to wait.

Pricing

Many individuals mess up when it comes to pricing. Like any other business, you need to leave your sentiments and emotions. It would be best if you put them aside for something else. I have seen tons of cars that are far too overpriced either because the owner thinks that their car is worth more or because it is their only means of transportation if you're renting out the same car you're using get around.

Make sure you price your car manually. You have a feature used to auto price your car based on market data, but do not use that!

When you initially list your car, it will automatically default to this option! Keep the price of your cars consistent.

Their market data tool is excellent but doesn't work well if everyone else is listing their cars for $90 and you want to list yours for $40.

It is also pretty hard to undercut the market when you can't get a good deal on a car. For our first few cars, we leased them. Negotiating a good deal from the start is extremely important to the success of your soon to be rental empire! For example, a high-end sports car can easily rent for $120/per day, but to maximize your profits, you shouldn't have a monthly payment of over $1,000. The idea behind this is that you want to make more money per month on the car than it depreciates, so you can also sell it in the coming months.

They are charging less than the market is the key to making a ton of money on your business.

Like I stated earlier, I have seen people list their Civics and other types of cars for around $90/per day, which a more realistic price for a car like that is $30-$40/per day.

If you're able to obtain a vehicle and rent it for that amount, chances are your car will be rented around 22+ days per month. People will also frequent your rentals more often, and you'll get a bunch of repeated renters.

Knowing what car to list is crucial when it comes to car renting. To do this, you'll need to do some research in the area that you live in.

The best performing cars at the moment are mid-size, large SUVs and luxury sports cars.

However, if you live in the United States, the chances are that no one will rent a large SUV. Be smart about your surroundings.

You'll also want to check out the current listings' prices and see if you can charge less than them by a lot.

In my opinion, to live a 9-to-5 free lifestyle, I often look to scale up different ideas to their maximum potential. Most people know me for presentations that I give on Manufactured Spending, but the truth is that there is more to me than it meets the eye.

Conclusion

Passive income streams are crucial to designing your portfolio because they can generate predictable income with little to no maintenance, diversify your portfolio, and increase your overall cash flow. Those who are the most successful are those who have the most control over their time. The more work you put into generating passive income streams, the more control you will have over your precious time in the long run. Passive income is most relative to what you want to offer. Whether it's a product or your service, you can develop a substantial recurring income stream with the right tools in place. Once you realized that you could productize and create an automated income from it,

Passive income opportunities also bring you closer to financial freedom by earning you a supplemental income.

Most are, however, preceded by significant capital investments, dedication, and hourly contributions. Others like crypto and forex engagements expose your initial investments to enormous risks.

Therefore, you must consider these factors before deciding on the best passive income generation idea that you want to pursue or would like to pursue.

You do not have to sell physical products; there are plenty of other digital products you can create for next to nothing and sell them online. Almost no overheads are involved in this type of strategy.

If you're looking to sell a physical product online, consider services such as Shopify,eBay, Craigslist, and Etsy.

When it comes to getting started, there are multiple different types of strategies, including email marketing, SEO, affiliate marketing, online advertising, and freelancing.

Be wise when thinking of stocks, shares, and Forex trading. Make sure you do plenty of research and only spend money that you are willing to lose.

You don't need a large budget to start; you can create your portfolio and get products out there for free on social media platforms.

If you have access to the internet and a computer, you're completely capable of starting an online business financially independent.

FAQ

Does Passive Income Work?

Yes! Passive income is how more affluent individuals continue to build wealth. When you don't have money, you can leverage your time and effort to create other income streams that will grow into the future. As you accumulate money, you can deploy that money (and even combine it with your time) to generate more and more passive income for the future/or future generations.

Does passive income require "no work"?

Passive income always requires something upfront: your time or money. However, the idea is that it becomes passive after you do more challenging work, alluring about it. For example, you spend six months writing a book, and then you can enjoy the royalty income from your book for the rest of your life without any further work. That's not to say that you cannot do more work to boost your income, but an element requires nothing more to earn.

What Are the Most Popular Passive Income Ideas?

The most popular include investing in the stock market, owning real estate, investing in a business, and only keeping your money in a high yield savings account. All of these approaches generate passive income automatically, but they do require upfront capital. And of course, there are lots of other popular passive income ideas.

Where Can I Invest to Have Passive Income?

If you need a safer approach, you can invest in a money market account or CD ladder to get a risk-free return on your money. If you want to invest in generating passive income, dividend stocks and mutual funds are great ways to do that. You can also invest in debt instruments, like bonds as well.

What Are Some Examples of Passive Income?

You can invest your money in company stock, and then you receive a dividend payment and appreciation on your investment. Another famous example is real estate. You can buy a property, and you enjoy the rent as passive income. Investing is an excellent example of passive income.

Why Are Passive Income Streams Important?

Generating passive income streams can be one of the best investments of both, and eventually leading to your financial freedom is greater control over your time, which is essential to all of us.

Time is the most important and valuable resource. That we're all given a finite amount, and, unlike most resources, it cannot be recovered. To maximize your potential for this precious resource, we must be wise about how we invest in both our time and hard-earned money.

CPSIA information can be obtained
at www.ICGtesting.com
Printed in the USA
LVHW010453140521
687424LV00003B/240